Magic M

The Truth About Psilocybin: An Introductory Guide to Shrooms, Psychedelic Mushrooms, and the Full Effects

presentation of the information is without contract or any type of guarantee assurance.

The trademarks that are used are without any consent, and the publication of the trademark is without permission or backing by the trademark owner. All trademarks and brands within this book are for clarifying purposes only and are owned by the owners themselves, not affiliated with this document.

Table of Contents

Introduction

You've probably heard about Magic Mushrooms some time before. Maybe you've heard about how they are supposed to give people who use them some semblance of euphoria and how they can somehow alter one's way of thinking. However, what exactly are psilocybin mushrooms, also known as Magic Mushrooms?

Well, in this short and concise book, we will get into the history of Psilocybin, the science behind Psilocybin, and how it can affect one's body. Most practically, we will also look at the pros and cons of this substance and how Psilocybin compares to other similar "drugs".

In this book we are aiming to look at this topic in an unbiased light. We are not promoting the consumption of mushrooms, per se, but we want to make sure that if someone is interested in this controversial topic, they can reach more informed conclusions.

We hope that you are able to learn a thing or two!

Chapter 1:

What Are Psilocybin Mushrooms?

Psilocybin Mushrooms, more popularly known as *"Magic Mushrooms"* or *"Shrooms"* are often used as recreational drugs, as an entheogen, which are substances that are used for spiritual or religious purposes, much like Marijuana for Rastafaris.

There are over 100 species of Psilocybin Mushrooms in the world, which includes *Psilocybe, Pluteus, Pholiotina, Panaeolus, Mycena, Inocybe*, and *Galerina*.

Psilocybin and Synesthesia

Psilocybin Mushrooms could give someone spiritual experiences and may even alter his/her sense of time. More so, it is shown that Psilocybin causes synesthesia, which means that one's cognitive and sensory pathways are altered. For example, when one is in synesthesia, he/she won't see colors the way most people do. In short, there would be so many changes around them that they would cause them to feel like they are having an "out of body experience."

More so, when one is in synesthesia, his/her experiences may vary from what others experience in that same state. A person may or may not be aware of it, and this is why scientific research on the subject is limited at this time.

Examples of Synesthesia:

Lexical-Gustatory
This means that one could taste something just by hearing words, for example when someone hears the word couches and he/she immediately thinks that couches taste like cakes.

Mirror-Touch
It's almost the same as empathy, or when someone literally feels what someone else feels. It is said that this is mostly caused by mirror neurons in one's brain and body.

Misophonia
This is one of the negative effects of synesthesia where specific sounds trigger negative emotions, such as disgust, hatred, anger, and fright.

Ordinal Linguistic Personification
When someone experiences this it means that he/she is able to connect letters, months, days, and numbers to certain personalities, and this has been recorded since the 1890's.

Auditory-Tactile

Auditory-Tactile Synesthesia literally means that sensations in one's body are induced because of certain sounds.

Number Form
This form of synesthesia occurs when a person suddenly sees numbers or numerical images in his/her head simply by thinking about said numbers.

Spatial-Sequence
This is when people tend to say that one number is closer than the other simply by thinking about them.

Chromestesia
Chromestesia is the term given to an experience whereby a person associates colors with sounds, which may be triggered by talking, listening to music, or other sound effects.

Grapheme-Color
Finally, this form of synesthesia is about thinking that numbers and letters are actually tinted by colors, and these colors will always be connected to those colors.

One interesting thing about synesthesia, though, is the fact that some people are able to apply their synesthetic experiences to their daily lives. It's like they get to feel like they have these hidden senses within them, and this somehow makes them feel like they can do things that they otherwise couldn't.

Chapter 2:

History of Psilocybin

So, when was it exactly that Psilocybin became prevalent on earth?

How it all began

Well, the history of Psilocybin can be traced back to the earliest days on earth, even as early as 5000 B.C. This is evident in the fact that there are ancient artifacts, such as paintings and sculptures, which have been found in Northern Algeria's Tassili

Plateau. These paintings depict how early humans used mushrooms for recreational purposes.

More so, there also have been mushroom stones found in some caves in Central and South America, especially in Mexico. If you are not aware, the history of Mexico has a lot to do with worshipping gods and various deities. One of these gods is someone named 7 Flower (Piltzentecutchi) and was also deemed as the god of hallucinatory plants. Depictions of 7 Flower often connected him to the so-called *Divine Mushroom*, alongside using mushrooms with some other gods.

Meanwhile, the Aztecs also had who they called the Prince of the Flowers, who was also known as the god of psychoactive plants, which they all considered sacred. They believed that by worshipping the Prince of the Flowers, they'd experience flowery dreams, especially if they get to use mushrooms. Aside from mushrooms, they also used *Peyote, Datura*, and *Morning Glory*, to get into psychoactive trances. They mostly used these for their religious rituals, most especially after the Aztecs defeated Cortez in 1521. During this phase, they called Psilocybin the *Wondrous Mushrooms.*

There was even a scheduled plan that they followed in consuming those mushrooms. First, they wanted to be drunk so they had to eat the black mushrooms first, and before dawn, they ate smaller mushrooms with honey to induce hallucinations. Upon feeling the effects that the mushrooms brought upon them, they would begin to sing and dance all around the room. They experienced a wide range of emotions during these experiences, and some would even weep intensely for hours on end. Oftentimes, many of the participants would get together and discuss their experiences after the effects had tapered.

Over time, Aztec Priests continued to use these mushrooms in their religious rituals, mostly because they could just find these mushrooms in their vicinity. However, in the early 20th century, Western Academics started to doubt that these things were real, and some thought that they weren't because they believed that *Peyotes* were not mushrooms.

However, after many experts spent years of researching the history and progression of human beings in certain parts of the world, these doubts were put to rest.

A New Twist to Christmas?

There are some stories that say that Siberian Shamans used hallucinogenic mushrooms as gifts to those who lived in their area during the Christmas or winter seasons.

John Rush, an anthropologist from the College of Sierra, once said that the reason why kids wait for flying elves and Santa Claus on Christmas Eve is because of this tradition that the Shamans started. As for reindeer, they were considered as the Shaman's spirit animals.

When the Shamans ingested mushrooms, they were convinced that these animals could actually fly, so they also imagined someone like Santa Claus because of the red and white colors that the mushrooms produced in their brains.

In Modern Times

In 1799, the *London Medical and Physical Journal* mentioned hallucinogenic mushrooms because a boy picked up some mushrooms from the Green Park in London and, upon using them, his parents noticed that he just began laughing without any reason, and it was as if he couldn't hear them talking to him. This triggered many scientists and researchers in the area to begin looking into the effects of these mushrooms when ingested by humans.

Later, in the 1930's, an amateur Austrian anthropologist named Robert Weitlaner visited Oaxaca, Mexico and became a witness to a "Mazatec mushroom ceremony." He noticed how the villagers used the mushrooms for relaxation and was prompted to send samples of the mushrooms to his colleagues. Investigations continued for years until the Second World War temporarily disrupted it.

Then in 1953, a group of anthropologists led by R. Gordon Wasson traveled to Huatla de Jimenez in Mexico and were actually able to participate in a mushroom ceremony, being the first recorded Caucasians ever to do so. Wasson and his wife, Valentina, soon published a series of papers depicting the event. They also brought back samples of mushrooms, specifically the *Psilocybe* species to show to their colleagues, just as Weitlaner had done before.

This series of events consequently triggered an interest by many people throughout the world. Among these people includes Timothy Leary, who also went to Mexico to take part in a mushroom ceremony in 1960 and went to tell the tale at Harvard University, where he was studying at that point in time. He also started the Harvard Psilocybin Project with his good friend Richard Alpert. However, this prompted Harvard officials to dismiss them from school, as some people believed that they promoted the use of psychedelic and recreational drugs because of the *Hippie Culture* of the 1960s.

However, their dismissal wasn't in vain. In fact, it prompted others to start using Psilocybin Mushrooms for recreational purposes, especially during the 1970's. More books on the subject were written, and these mushrooms are still heavily used in some parts of Mexico until this very day today. Some who live in Mexico have attributed their usage as homage to *Maria Sabina,* a local who planted and used Psilocybin Mushrooms all throughout her life, until her death in 1985. Sabina also believed that the mushrooms could offer a range of medicinal properties as well.

Needless to say, these mushrooms sure have a colorful history behind them, whether it is the length of time that they were "undiscovered" by the Western

World or their suppression once they were discovered, and that is one of the reasons why so many people are curious about these fascinating tools, even if they have no interest in using them personally.

Chapter 3:

The Science Behind Psilocybin

Of course, Psilocybin Mushrooms wouldn't be able to do any of the effects that people have attributed to them if there were no scientific processes involved. In this chapter, you will learn more about the science behind Psilocybin.

First and foremost, we have to understand that Psilocybin occurs as a psychedelic compound in more than 200 species of mushrooms. You can find the most potent ones in the Psilocybe species, as mentioned earlier, and as evident in the fact that early Mexicans often preferred Psilocybes more than any other species of mushrooms that they had access to.

A Pro-Drug

Psilocybin is a Pro-Drug. This means that, as a medication, it is administered in an inactive form to be effective. This does not necessarily mean that it has medicinal purposes though. However, it does mean that it can enhance the benefits of medicine that you are taking. This is because a Pro-Drug is a precursor of a drug, so it could essentially improve the benefits that you will readily receive from medicines, particularly in chemotherapy and other important treatments.

Psilocybin is considered to be a Type II Pro-Drug, which means that it is activated outside the cells. It also means that it mixes well with blood and that it could work with other bodily fluids during circulation.

When Psilocybin enters the body, it is transformed into Psilocin. Psilocin is known as a serotonergic psychedelic substance, which is also tryptamine alkaloid, and can alter the effects of other drugs, such as DMT and LSD. In other words, this means that Psilocybin doesn't enter the human body as itself but as its cousin, Psilocin.

Moreover, the possible reason why synesthesia occurs and the fact that it differs for everyone is the fact that Psilocin isn't stable and has no permanent effect to Dopamine receptors, amongst others. Its life only ranges for around one to three hours, so effects would no longer be very prevalent after the said time frame.

Perceptual Distortions

The science behind Psilocybin also has a lot to do with perceptual distortions. The tool alters the passage of time for most people, making it faster or slower than it actually is. This is mainly because of a temporary impairment caused by Psilocin that could alter time by around 2.5 seconds.

You can connect this activity to how Psilocybin affects the Prefrontal Cortex, which is the part of the brain that works behind attention, memory, and brain imaging. Because of this, synesthesia happens. There are also debates as to how the neurochemical elements behind Psilocybin have something to do with this, which could also lead one to realize that:

1. Synesthesia certainly affects the brain, and it happens automatically and involuntarily;

2. The effects are generic and consistent, and;

3. Sense of location is one of the main examples of how Psilocybin affects the brain.

There is a lot of cross talking that happens between different brain regions, which then causes synesthesia. Some even say that it has a lot to do with uninhibited feedback, which means that the brain works in such a way that it gives you reactions and feedback that are far from the usual (hence, you see colors differently, you think numbers are tinted, etc.) The feedback could then influence the way the brain and, even your vision, works.

Some scientists have also linked the effects of Psilocybin to what happens in the brains of Schizophrenics. However, there is much debate as to whether this is true or not. And, speaking of the effects of Psilocybin, you'll learn more about this in the following chapter…

Chapter 4:

The Effects of Psilocybin

As previously stated, Psilocybin can really do a lot with the brain. What you should first keep in mind is that the effects are often at their peak during the first three to four hours of usage, and then those effects can last for one to three more hours. However, some people say that they feel the effects for up to eight hours. So, again, it differs for everyone.

Emotional

When it comes to the emotional effects of the mushrooms, it often depends on the setting. Some users have said that it is better to use the mushrooms when one is in a laid-back environment so that his/her brain won't go elsewhere. Familiar environments are also good, as long as a person is comfortable with them. Once a person is in a place where he feels like he doesn't belong, he might suffer from anxiety during the "trip," which can oftentimes be unpleasant for the tripper. So, the number one rule (according to most experienced trippers) is to make sure that you go enjoy your "trip" somewhere safe - somewhere you are familiar with.

Sensory

Psilocybin can affect tactile, visual, and auditory senses more than others. These are usually felt after 30 minutes of ingesting the mushrooms. Possibly the first things one would experience is seeing trails behind some objects that are moving, a sense that the environment is melting, strange halos, auras, light phenomena, contrasting of colors, and color enhancement.

Synesthesia is also a big product of the sensory effects of Psilocybin. You can read about that again in the first chapter of this book.

Spiritual

As mentioned earlier, Psilocybin is still an important part of certain religious sects and civilizations, especially in Mexico. Depending on one's beliefs, Psilocybin could be considered to be religious, as well as a sacrament.

When one uses mushrooms for spiritual trances, it is said that a person is able to enter realms that he/she has never been to before. Additionally, it can cause that person to reaffirm his/her values from that realm. However, it is often cited as a tool that can improve cohesion for a certain group, especially with groups in which members already believe in the power of these mushrooms.

Conscious states are induced and the effects might be prevalent for a while. This is the reason why it is often used in "Mysticism" and why people consider these mushrooms as means to get to mystical states. They sometimes believe that the mushrooms enhance their philosophies and ways of thinking and that they help them get closer to the gods—or whatever Supreme Being they believe in. In fact, some people consider the time they are able to use Psilocybin Mushrooms as the most important part of their spiritual lives. Some also believe that the mushrooms work against anxiety and depression and there is certainly a case to be made here, though these claims are usually empirical.

Medicinal

Research is still being done as to how Psilocybin can help people medically. However, there are some cases in which Psilocybin was able to stop OCD and even clinical depression for some patients, so one can say that it has positive effects for the brain and could actually work as an anti-depressant.

Chapter 5:

Pros and Cons of Psilocybin

As always, there are pros and cons to anything —
including Psilocybin!

Pros

Here are some of the best things about Psilocybin:

It causes less, if not, absolutely no damage.

According to surveys made in the U.S. and the UK,
most recreational drug users have said that Psilocybin
is indeed safer than other recreational drugs that they
have tried because it is not toxic to the organs of the
body.

New connections between neurons are made.

Do you know what this does? It actually lessens the risk of Dementia and Alzheimer's. Typically, when a person gets older, his/her neurons tend to move away from each other and could no longer communicate. Although, if he uses Psilocybin, then there's a big chance that those neurons could reconnect with each other, so such a person would have a much better change at accessing their memories.

It may help smokers quit smoking.

Some researches show that smokers who have tried using mushrooms have eventually given up on smoking because the mushrooms were able to calm them down, especially when they use them while listening to music.

The mushrooms can kill fear.

There is a connection between the depletion of anxiety and depression - meaning that fear might be killed when one ingests these mushrooms. Research has shown that a person is less likely to freeze up or have racing heartbeats when he or she is placed in an unlikely situation after using the mushrooms. This is also the reason why the mushrooms are being studied so they could hopefully be used to treat a broad range of mental conditions in the future.

It allows information to travel freely in the brain.

Here's the thing: Psilocybin slows down the activity of the thalamus. In other words, brain communication processes are enhanced, so information would be able to travel freely, leading a person to be able to think more clearly. It wouldn't limit that person from processing information, especially when that person might feel like the information wasn't supposed to be there to begin with. In turn, this process makes your brain "work" more, and when this happens, it could prevent Alzheimer's and Dementia.

It hyper-connects the brain.

Psilocybin boosts other activity in the brain, which again can be very healthy. The mushrooms work in a placebo effect kind of way by waking up parts of the brain that aren't always working, which could certainly make a person more coherent and intelligent. In fact, some experienced users have said that it has helped them with lucid dreaming.

It may change someone for the better.

It may seem unlikely to some who are ignorant to this phenomenon but it's actually true. It may not happen right away, but research has expressed that Psilocybin users have managed to change their behavior for the better in just a matter of 14 months. This is especially true in the cases of people who are creative, open to change, or have liberal points of view on life (not in the political sense, but rather as a term for "open to fluid ways of thinking"). Some have considered the trips as profound experiences, and that is the main reason why they choose to do it instead of looking to alcohol or other drugs.

Cons

As with anything that we put in or on our body, we must be very aware of the possible negative effects of Psilocybin mushrooms. Here are some things you must be aware of:

It may induce Hallucinogen Persisting Perception Disorder (HPPD).

One of the main things that one should be aware of when it comes to using Psilocybin is the fact that it may induce HPPD, a condition that is characterized by sensory disturbances. Of course, because synesthesia is one of the effects of Psilocybin, there is the problem that it may cause this condition. One piece of evidence is the fact that users sometimes suffer from flashbacks, even in hours after using the mushrooms. However, this doesn't happen to the majority. In fact, only around 4.1% of users suffer from it, but it's still best to be aware of this.

Mood Swings
This is another effect that happens because of HPPD. If one is diagnosed with it, he/she can expect that

there will be some minor to intense mood swings, based on the intensity and duration of the flashbacks.

Prolonged Derealization
Another problem might be the fact that the user may feel like his/her realizations come a little too late or that they don't get to give out their opinions when they are asked to. Somehow, some users have experienced being derailed from reality for a longer time than expected, and of course, this isn't good because it could disrupt the way they work or their daily lifestyle, in general.

Panic Attacks
Incidentally, some people who have used Psilocybin have said that they suffered from panic attacks, which could be a bit confusing because it is also said that Psilocybin has a lot to do with depleting anxiety. This area is being researched to find what the possible benefits of Psilocybin on people with anxiety could be, as well as how the negative kickbacks can be avoided or minimized. As for now, it is something that we all must be aware of.

Convulsions/Paranoia
There's also a 1 to 2% bracket of people who have said that they've become quite paranoid when they

are not using the mushrooms or just hours after using them.

Vision Problems

Lastly, there are around 2% of users who have said that they felt as if their vision was affected by the usage of Psilocybin. However, even they aren't sure whether the vision problems have something to do with Psilocybin or that maybe they are just having vision and spatial problems because of adverse effects of the mushrooms, so further research still needs to be done. Nevertheless, it cannot be denied that Psilocybin actually has an affect on the eyes, most especially the retina, at least for a short period of time or while the user is still tripping.

Chapter 6:

Psilocybin Compared to Other Drugs

Of course, there will always be the issue of Psilocybin being compared to other drugs, especially by the general public, those who have no experience with "drugs" or know anybody who does.

On Marijuana

Let's start with the similarities. Psilocybin and Marijuana are both heavily rooted to religious and spiritual traditions. While the Aztecs have Psilocybin, Rastafaris have Marijuana. So, one can both connect them to nature and to how a culture is depicted, at least where history is concerned.

They are both linked to experiencing spiritual profoundness and experiencing new "realms" within the mind. One could say that synesthesia is also evident to users of Marijuana. They also experience sensory distortions, especially when it comes to visual and spatial effects. Some users of both drugs have said that they have experienced an alteration of colors and felt like they are not really where they are.

However, they have their differences, of course. For one, Marijuana has to be bred before being used. There are also various ways of preparing it, such as wax, tincture, hash, or Kief. On the other hand, Psilocybin could grow by itself because it is a wild mushroom.

Psilocybin can produce its own spores, which means that they could grow by themselves and grow wherever the wind takes them. That is why they are prevalent in a lot of areas in Mexico. They also have a lot to do with the way water vapor works because spores could be lifted up by the air, making them important in the ecological process of the regions they inhabit.

Moreover, Marijuana is actually already legal in some states and countries as part of their medicinal programs. In this case, it's called Cannabis. Of course, not everyone agrees to this, but it is still one big leap from Marijuana being treated as a deadly drug before. In some parts of the world, Marijuana is also legal for recreational purposes — a feat that mushrooms still have not achieved because, in a way, they are still considered as novices in the legal and medicinal domain.

On DMT

Another drug that Psilocybin is often compared to is DMT, which is mainly used for recreational purposes as opposed to having any major medicinal benefits (as of this publication).

Users have said that the duration of the effects of DMT only last for around 30 minutes, with 30-second highs and another 30 minutes of after-effects, which could be a bit inconvenient for a lot of people. They liken the effects of DMT to experiencing Acid Trips for around an hour or so.

What makes DMT even more inconvenient is the fact that a person may not be able to move for around 15 seconds or so and his/her visual senses will be thoroughly affected, at least while they are tripping. The user won't feel connected to who they are and where they currently are. Oftentimes, they will not be able to articulate what they experienced while being on the trip. So, if they want to remember what they experienced in the future, they are better off writing down what is happening during or directly after the trip.

On LSD (Acid)

LSD probably will make you experience a lot of things in a 45-minute to 2-hour period, depending on how much you have taken. Basically, you will really be on a "high" while on this drug and you might be in a fit of giggles before you know it. In a matter of 3 minutes or so, you can already be experiencing this. As time goes by, you will usually notice that the visuals will be more and more altered and confusing and colors can be extremely different from what you deemed they would be.

LSD may also make you suffer from social anxiety, extreme mood swings, and may get you thinking philosophically. While you are on LSD, though, you may find it easy to make art, listen to music, harness your skills, and you may also feel the need to analyze your life and the relationships that you have, or had. The effects weaken after around five to seven hours from ingesting. LSD is also said to be the kind of drug that is best for doing with your friends.

On Mescaline

Now, Mescaline is way, way different than the other drugs mentioned because it doesn't have the same spiritual effects and hits a person in such a way that it would numb them down and make them feel warm inside, but not the kind of warmth that you usually feel when you are extremely comfortable and such.

The person will also feel like their field of vision is being blocked and may also feel like the entire world has changed. Soon after the trip, a person might feel confused and in a mental haze. More so, some users have admitted that they threw up four hours after using the said drug, so if you often feel dizzy and don't like the texture of new things on your mouth, then you might as well not try this one out.

Chapter 7:

The Future of Psilocybin

So, what does the future hold for Psilocybin?

Well, you can say that there are still a lot of people in the world who don't know what Psilocybin can do. Legalities are not clear in some countries, but then again, you really can not stop them from growing and materializing, simply because they are mushrooms. They are the kind of plants that would keep on growing despite basic efforts against it, and because they are a big part of ancient Mexican and Siberian Culture, you really cannot expect that they would be removed or outlawed completely without outrage from people who still use them as part of their lifestyle.

Cultural Differences

But, really, is it a bad thing that they keep on growing? Could someone be considered a drug addict by using Psilocybin?

If you've been reading this book thoroughly, then you have realized by now that there is really nothing wrong with it. After all, it could bring someone closer to spiritual realms that he/she never thought were around before. It could also invoke in them the chance to feel like he/she is not alone in this world and that this world is so much more than what they originally thought.

Another thing would be the fact that because it is connected to ancient cultures and that it has a lot to do with religious and spiritual processes, it has a sacred place in many people's life, so it couldn't just be dismissed as something that should be banned. We have to remember that things like this have to be respected, that none of us own this world and that these natural processes were around before us and will most likely be around after us.

The Medicinal Benefits

So, what about the medicinal benefits?

Sure, not everything is scientifically accepted right now but there really is quite a bit of evidence that shows how Psilocybin could alter one's mind in a positive manner. After all, it's a recreational drug, so it could be used while being in control of one's faculties. In a case like this, it is the person's responsibility to know whether or not he/she should stop or go on using something.

Plus, there is also the fact that it could enhance someone's spatial knowledge and skills. It could make someone feel happy, even for a brief period of time, and if he/she remembers this, then it might be much easier for him/her to live. A person who is has spent years in depression might not be aware of such peak states of happiness because of the downward spiral that their life circumstances have forced them into.

As for what you have read here, mushrooms could help someone overcome, and may even prevent, medical conditions such as Dementia and Alzheimer's, which is something that simply cannot be ignored (similar to how Marijuana has gained traction as a medicine for major diseases).

What only needs to be done now is to make sure that proper research is done and that people don't just take for granted the fact that Psilocybin might be good for one's health. Sure, it's not what's been and is being taught in school, but one cannot always say that everything that is being taught in school is the right thing. It's always best to open one's mind to the reality of the world - that there are certain things out there that could be good for one's health, yet not a lot of people know about them.

The Future

Where does it go from here?

While some countries in the world are still not open to using Psilocybin for medicinal purposes, there is a big chance that a time will come and this will happen. After all, if Marijuana is now legalized in some countries and states, then why can't Psilocybin be?

One only needs to open up their eyes to see that the world is so much more than what one might have been taught by authority figures while growing up and that Psilocybin could change one's life for the better. With self-control, and with an open mind, Psilocybin could lead someone to new, unchartered paths—paths that will surely make him/her understand themselves and the world even more.

With that said, the future might just be great for these mushrooms, after all.

Conclusion

Thank you for reading this! We hope this short, concise book was able to teach you a thing or two about Magic Mushrooms.

Now that you understand the important factors regarding Psilocybin, you can decide if you want to try it, or if you can inform your friends who ask you about it. Plus, a little addition to your knowledge doesn't hurt, right? Our world is becoming increasingly interested in the use of Mushrooms and other psychedelic substances, in hopes to enhance the human experience on Earth.

If you've learned anything from this book, please take the time to share your thoughts by sending me a personal message, or even posting a review on Amazon. It would be greatly appreciated and I try my best to get back to every message!

Thank you and good luck in your journey!

Printed in Great Britain
by Amazon